THE PHILOSOPHY OF A HOMEMADE EDUCATION

Copyright

The Philosophy of a Homemade Education. Copyright © 2025 by Shelby Dersa. All rights reserved. No part of this book may be used or reproduced in any manner whatsoever without written permission. While the author and publisher have used their best efforts in preparing this book, they make no representations or warranties with this book. The advice and strategies contained herein may not be suitable for your situation or location. You should always first consult with a professional regarding the homeschool laws in your state of residency. Neither the publisher or the author shall be liable for any wrongdoing on behalf of a parent or guardian when deciding to homeschool their children.

For information, please email ahomemadeeducation@gmail.com or visit http://ahomemadeeducationpress.com

Paperback edition published by A Homemade Education Press in 2025.

Designed by Shelby Dersa
Cover and interior images: Canva

ISBN: 979-8-9882547-5-1

Other Books by the Author

Table of Contents

Chapter 1: Home Culture..8

Chapter 2: Rebel Against the System............................14

Chapter 3: The Socialization Theory.............................22

Chapter 4: Revamp Childhood..30

Chapter 5: The Nitty-Gritty of Homeschooling............36

Chapter 6: Preschool-Second Grade Academics.............46

Chapter 7: Third Grade-Fifth Grade Academics............66

Chapter 8: Middle School Academics............................80

Chapter 9: Enrichment Studies 88

Chapter 10: High School & Graduation...,......................98

Chapter 11: Create a Homemade Education.................116

A HOMEMADE EDUCATION

The ideology behind the movement of A Homemade Education started with a mom who saw the beauty of bringing her children back home in regard to the public school system. As a kid, she grew up in that system. She saw the positives and the negatives, the stressors and the strengths, and the good and bad effects it had on mental well-being. She carried her experiences with her up until she had children herself. When they started attending school, the same occurrences began happening to them too. From bullying and exclusion to endless homework and not much family time left to spare, her kids dreaded school altogether.

One day, while dropping her child off at school, he refused to step out of the car. "What's wrong?" she asked. He just looked down and wept. "I don't want to go in there," he responded through tears. That is the year she brought her second child home to be home educated. That is also the year she started the A Homemade Education page on social media. She posted about her thoughts on homeschooling, her experiences with her children, and tips and advice. While followers of the page increased, her philosophy became popular with parents and so did her books. From inspiring parents to slow down, live more simply, and preserve childhood, she was on a mission to show how homeschooling promoted that type of lifestyle. A Homemade Education is not a teaching method, a curriculum, or a technique... it's a philosophy.

ONE:

HOME CULTURE

It Starts and Ends at Home

Our culture has undergone a remarkable transformation through the ages. Once, the home stood as the sacred sanctuary where children thrived—learning, playing, and absorbing influences. Now, the prevailing belief champions the early release of children from their familial havens. It is thought that fostering independence, socialization, and new skills should occur in the absence of parental figures, beginning as early as the tender age of three.

Many experts advocate for placing children into the welcoming embrace of strangers as frequently as possible, whether through daycares, social gatherings, or preschools. They so desperately want to separate a child's identity from their home life, but why? No matter how old a person becomes, home is the foundation for their life. There is nothing wrong with embracing the utmost important place that makes them who they are. However, today's way of thinking in modern society is trying to convince people otherwise, taking away the importance of family values, the family support system, and straining relationships.

Indoctrination

I often read comments online from opposers of homeschooling who like to criticize parents for doing so. Something that has stood out the most to me are the people who accuse others of indoctrinating their children by homeschooling them. Their thoughts are that home-educated children will only be surrounded by their own parents' beliefs, mindsets, and knowledge, and in return, they are not adequately exposed to the outside world to form their own opinions about various aspects of life. There are two issues with this notion.

The first is that society still thinks that homeschoolers do not leave their homes. Homeschool parents actively seek new experiences for their children to make up for the fact that they are not attending a traditional school and to take them out of their comfort zones of a home environment.

Issue number two is that many think that a family that spends too much time together will negatively influence the children. It is every parent's job to influence their own children. It is not everyone else's job to decide how they go

Other Books by the Author

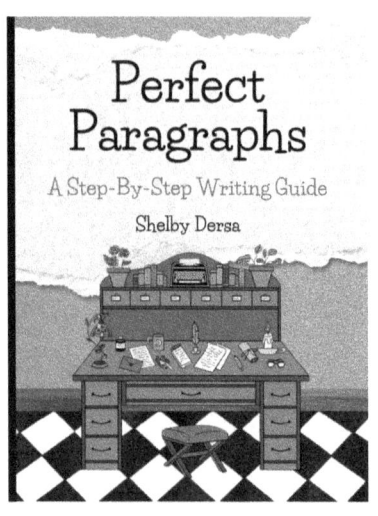

and adequately support their needs. As a homeschool parent, you are capable of giving your child the one-on-one attention they crave and that they also require. You know them better than any other person on this Earth, and therefore you have the natural instinct to nurture their growth by supporting strengths, working through weaknesses, and challenging them at their unique level. That is something children would not otherwise receive from anywhere but at home.

YOU DON'T HAVE TO BE A PERFECT HOMESCHOOL PARENT. YOU JUST HAVE TO BE WILLING TO LEARN ALONGSIDE THEM.

The Importance of Conversation

When people think of homeschooling, they might picture the parent standing over her kids, directing what to do.

about it.

If we lived in a country that suddenly put restraints on every decision a parent makes, then we would not live in a free country. It is baffling that any American would wish to banish the right of other parents that allows them to choose how to educate their children. Who knows, it could end up backfiring on them and their own decisions as well.

IF ONE WISHES TO BANISH HOMESCHOOLING, THEN THEY WISH TO BANISH FREEDOM.

Parents are Natural Teachers

Whether you grew up with the ability to teach educational concepts to others or not, parents are usually natural teachers to their own children. How well a parent can teach that child does not have much to do with their academic background, as some may think. It's more about the willingness to learn alongside their child, guide them,

ONE:

HOME CULTURE

her experiences with her children, and tips and advice. While followers of the page increased, her philosophy became popular with parents and so did her books. From inspiring parents to slow down, live more simply, and preserve childhood, she was on a mission to show how homeschooling promoted that type of lifestyle. A Homemade Education is not a teaching method, a curriculum, or a technique... it's a philosophy.

A HOMEMADE EDUCATION

The ideology behind the movement of A Homemade Education started with a mom who saw the beauty of bringing her children back home in regard to the public school system. As a kid, she grew up in that system. She saw the positives and the negatives, the stressors and the strengths, and the good and bad effects it had on mental well-being. She carried her experiences with her up until she had children herself. When they started attending school, the same occurrences began happening to them too. From bullying and exclusion to endless homework and not much family time left to spare, her kids dreaded school altogether.

One day, while dropping her child off at school, he refused to step out of the car. "What's wrong?" she asked. He just looked down and wept. "I don't want to go in there," he responded through tears. That is the year she brought her second child home to be home educated. That is also the year she started the A Homemade Education page on social media. She posted about her thoughts on homeschooling,

Table of Contents

Chapter 1: Home Culture..8

Chapter 2: Rebel Against the System............................14

Chapter 3: The Socialization Theory.............................22

Chapter 4: Revamp Childhood..30

Chapter 5: The Nitty-Gritty of Homeschooling............36

Chapter 6: Preschool-Second Grade Academics.............46

Chapter 7: Third Grade-Fifth Grade Academics............66

Chapter 8: Middle School Academics.............................80

Chapter 9: Enrichment Studies 88

Chapter 10: High School & Graduation....,.....................98

Chapter 11: Create a Homemade Education.................116

Copyright

The Philosophy of a Homemade Education. Copyright © 2025 by Shelby Dersa. All rights reserved. No part of this book may be used or reproduced in any manner whatsoever without written permission. While the author and publisher have used their best efforts in preparing this book, they make no representations or warranties with this book. The advice and strategies contained herein may not be suitable for your situation or location. You should always first consult with a professional regarding the homeschool laws in your state of residency. Neither the publisher or the author shall be liable for any wrongdoing on behalf of a parent or guardian when deciding to homeschool their children.

For information, please email ahomemadeeducation@gmail.com or visit http://ahomemadeeducationpress.com

Paperback edition published by A Homemade Education Press in 2025.

Designed by Shelby Dersa
Cover and interior images: Canva

ISBN: 979-8-9882547-5-1

THE PHILOSOPHY OF A HOMEMADE EDUCATION

It Starts and Ends at Home

Our culture has undergone a remarkable transformation through the ages. Once, the home stood as the sacred sanctuary where children thrived—learning, playing, and absorbing influences. Now, the prevailing belief champions the early release of children from their familial havens. It is thought that fostering independence, socialization, and new skills should occur in the absence of parental figures, beginning as early as the tender age of three.

Many experts advocate for placing children into the welcoming embrace of strangers as frequently as possible, whether through daycares, social gatherings, or preschools. They so desperately want to separate a child's identity from their home life, but why? No matter how old a person becomes, home is the foundation for their life. There is nothing wrong with embracing the utmost important place that makes them who they are. However, today's way of thinking in modern society is trying to convince people otherwise, taking away the importance of family values, the family support system, and straining relationships.

Indoctrination

I often read comments online from opposers of homeschooling who like to criticize parents for doing so. Something that has stood out the most to me are the people who accuse others of indoctrinating their children by homeschooling them. Their thoughts are that home-educated children will only be surrounded by their own parents' beliefs, mindsets, and knowledge, and in return, they are not adequately exposed to the outside world to form their own opinions about various aspects of life. There are two issues with this notion.

The first is that society still thinks that homeschoolers do not leave their homes. Homeschool parents actively seek new experiences for their children to make up for the fact that they are not attending a traditional school and to take them out of their comfort zones of a home environment.

Issue number two is that many think that a family that spends too much time together will negatively influence the children. It is every parent's job to influence their own children. It is not everyone else's job to decide how they go

Parents are not school teachers, though, and they are not meant to be. There is usually less instructing and more conversing going on around the table while they teach their children throughout their lessons. This educational dynamic is one that would only be seen in the home environment. As a result, children are able to actively engage in their education and see themselves as participants in their learning path, as opposed to just students who need to be taught by a more educated authority figure. This key skill will set the stage for a child to become a lifelong learner.

Connections

Individuals will come into your child's life who will teach them things, but it is likely that no one else has a connection to your child like you do. Your relationship is synchronized in a way that no one else understands. Their hurts and their joys, and their strengths and their weaknesses, are things that you are likely in tune with. This type of connection can be utilized to teach them the way they need to be taught.

TWO:

REBEL AGAINST THE SYSTEM

Not Better or Worse, Just Different

When things have been done the same way for so long, it's hard not to simply conform. Straying from the path more often taken can feel uneasy. Even so, many parents before you have taken the road less traveled until the very end. You are far from being the first to homeschool or even graduate your children through homeschooling.

Many ask themselves, "What if I mess up my kids?" The type of education a child receives will not ruin your child's life. Do you want to know what does have a potentially hurtful impact on it, though? Their environment. So if you are on the fence about homeschooling because you feel torn between where to educate your children, think of the environment you are willing to provide for them and how it differs from a traditional school. Consider their mental health, self-esteem, stressors, and positive social interactions. If you feel that a homeschool environment serves as a better place for your child, then you are making the right decision. Let go of feeling like you must choose what everyone else does. You're not taking anything away from your children.

You're just choosing to live life differently with them. You are rebelling against a system; let it liberate your family.

Homeschooling is Enough

Sometimes, parents have it in their heads that they will fail at homeschooling if they aren't doing "enough." When thinking about how a classroom is set up, the hours in a school day, and the amount of work, plus homework a typical child receives each day, it can put pressure on the homeschool parent to live up to these expectations.

There is a reason why a traditional classroom should not be copied in your homeschool. Classrooms were never meant to educate a few children at a time. They were set up with the idea that a larger number of children would be attending, and they needed to keep them busy for a certain number of hours each day. Homeschooling is not about keeping your children busy or logging a certain number of hours, even if it means throwing in meaningless tasks. It's about learning what you want to teach them, and that is it.

Learning Differences/Disabilities

If you have a child with learning differences or a disability, I can tell you that I know the decision to homeschool has weighed on you even more heavily than the average parent. That's because I've been there and I have gone through it from the beginning until the end.

Others might suggest leaving the teaching to the "experts" when discussing a child with different learning needs. What no one talks about, though, is how exactly a professional teacher is an expert when it comes to differences and disabilities. Teachers generally do not specialize in any other area besides general education. Their expertise is limited to their experiences. Special education teachers, of course, have specific training, but they are not always utilized to help certain children. For example, a child with ADHD most likely wouldn't receive special education services. A child with dyslexia might receive extra reading practice a couple of times per week if they are lucky. A child with autism may only receive help if they are on the severe end of the spectrum, and otherwise, there might be limited resources.

Special education and the help that is offered to children with learning differences or disabilities vary from school to school, from district to district, and even from state to state. Some might offer phenomenal help, but in many cases, the help is lacking. For example, specialized instruction, such as scientifically proven reading curriculum, is not offered in many schools across the country, despite the high numbers of students with dyslexia. In contrast, this type of curriculum can be purchased and used by any parent from the comfort of their home. Math programs that are more geared towards helping kids who struggle in this area or who have dyscalculia are available for purchase as well. Certain accommodations for ADHD or autism may not be available in a school setting but could be at home. The list goes on and on.

When considering whether or not to homeschool your child who has one of these differences or disabilities, I encourage you to thoroughly research what resources your child's potential school has. If you are at a loss because the school does seem to have very good services or methods to teach your child, but you still have a wish to homeschool, that doesn't mean you should stop considering it. Parents can obtain very good resources available to them as well, including curriculum that better fits their needs. Parents also have the ability to offer accommodations that simply do not exist in a traditional classroom.

WHEN A CHILD STRUGGLES AT SCHOOL, IT'S RECOMMENDED THAT THEY DO EVERYTHING THEY CAN TO CONFORM. HOMESCHOOLING RECOMMENDS THE OPPOSITE. THAT'S WHY IT MAKES SO MANY PEOPLE UNCOMFORTABLE.

Remember that homeschooling is kind of like specialized

education all by itself. There is no limit to how much of it can be customized to fit your child's needs. In my book *Homeschooling Wildflowers*, I dive deeper into the topic of homeschooling children with learning differences. From formulating a plan to home educate, to following through, I recommend reading it if your child has ADHD, dyslexia, dyscalculia, or dysgraphia.

Meet Them Where They Are

If teachers could stop right where each student is struggling and help them through it before moving forward for the rest of the class, think of the level of understanding that child would achieve. There would be no more gaps in their education. Now imagine what would happen if the teacher could stop repeating known information or skip unnecessary assignments for a single child. Think of how much further they could go in that area of study. Meeting children where they are instead of where they are supposed to be is one of the top reasons to choose home education.

The Schedule of Life

Living life differently can feel weird at first. You might ask yourself: "Is it bad that my kids sleep in until nine or ten? Does roller skating for five hours count as physical education for the week? Can we skip regular book work today and go for a walk in the forest for an immersive nature study instead? What about doing our school work in the evening so that we can meet up with friends at the park?" Yes, you can! The flexibility of homeschooling means that it can work around your family's lifestyle. Let go of the idea that your schedule must look a certain way or be similar to someone else's.

NEVER TRY TO CONVINCE SOMEONE WHO DOESN'T BELIEVE IN HOMESCHOOLING THAT IT IS GOOD. LET YOUR CHILD'S LIFE TELL THAT STORY.

THREE:

THE SOCIALIZATION THEORY

The Argument

Perhaps the greatest debate about homeschooling has nothing to do with the quality of education, but everything to do with the theory socialization. Both sides argue that one way of educating is better than the other because it provides the best environment for fostering social skills. Particularly, many believe that it would be detrimental to a child's social life to homeschool them. On the other side of the argument, some think that socialization shouldn't even be a topic that is discussed because traditional schooling does not promote socialization. We have all seen the memes about teachers telling students that the classroom is not the place for socializing, just to turn around and say that schools are needed for that exact reason. I'm sure that it is also possible that you have encountered comments about how people think homeschoolers are weird or socially awkward, while others say that they would rather have "weird" kids than products of the public school system.

I think we can all agree that children need to interact with children and adults who live outside of their own homes.

The question in this debate should not be, "Do children need socialization?" Of course they do. The focus of the argument should shift to the type of socialization children require, rather than questioning if they need it at all.

> **HOMESCHOOLERS ARE NOT WEIRD. THEY SIMPLY FEEL COMFORTABLE TRULY BEING THEMSELVES IN A WORLD WHERE CHILDREN FEEL PRESSURED TO BE LIKE THEIR PEERS, AND SOCIETY CONFUSES THE TWO.**

Socialization at School

Children spend six to seven hours each day in a school environment. With so much time spent with their peers, this should provide ample opportunity for interaction, friendship development, and social skill acquisition. However, the school system often overlooks the importance of utilizing this valuable time for socialization. Conversations are limited during class, lunch breaks are primarily for eating, and recess periods are relatively short. It's almost like schools are not the superior place to socialize. The truth is that rigor is of the highest importance within the school system. That fact is shown in the amount of chapter tests, homework, quizzes, state evaluations, and high school exams.

Different Environments

It is often believed that homeschoolers lack the exposure to new environments, that they are isolated, and that they are only around a set number of individuals. Society believes that as a result, they are closed off from the rest of the world.

When attending school, children are limited to the environment within the classroom. When homeschooled, the sky is the limit. One's home might be the base for learning, but exploring other avenues is usually not uncommon for homeschoolers. Whether they take classes at their local art studio, volunteer at a nursing home, or join a forest school during the warm months of summer, many are usually immersed in contrasting surroundings, exposing them to new experiences.

Diversity

Being homeschooled does not shield children from encountering individuals who differ from themselves. These children might often come from families steeped in rich beliefs, values, and identities, whether they are religious, secular, or adorned in alternative styles. They all have one thing in common, though: the steadfast belief in the transformative power of homeschooling and the cherished freedom to embrace the same path. Despite their differences, this type of education weaves a bond. These children are left with the wisdom of knowing how to engage with all walks of life.

Aside from meeting other homeschoolers who differ from themselves, let's not forget that they meet different kinds of people in different situations, just like anyone else would. Homeschooling doesn't take children away from the rest of the world; it puts them in it.

Community Involvement

The saying that the world is your oyster really is true for homeschoolers. The flexibility of time that they have to participate in activities allows for more community involvement that they otherwise wouldn't have available to them. Secondly, parents often seek out experiences that will enrich their children's education and social lives, leading them to these types of experiences. Whether it's volunteering at local shelters, participating in library clubs, or engaging in environmental projects, homeschoolers have the unique opportunity to tailor their schedules to include a variety of community-based activities. This not only enhances their learning but also instills a sense of responsibility and empathy. Additionally, many homeschooling families connect with community centers and local organizations, creating a network of support and collaboration that benefits both the students and the community. Through these experiences, children learn the value of giving back and develop a broader understanding of the world around them, preparing them for a future where they can actively contribute to society.

Homeschool Groups and Cooperatives

A wonderful aspect of homeschooling is the fact that parents who are involved in their children's education to this degree also mean most are willing to do the work to connect with other homeschoolers. Whether a parent starts a homeschool group of their own, volunteers for one, or drives their children an hour away to join a group of families, these parents make it happen. Groups can be informal, such as park-based meetings, nature clubs, or ones that get together to go on field trips. These are usually free to join. Formal groups can be large cooperatives with a board of directors or small with a few families who help organize them. These require a membership fee and possibly volunteering on the parents' end.

Groups and co-ops are a good option when wanting your children to connect with others who are in the same educational situation, but they are not always necessary.

Don't Underestimate Family

Many children grow up with childhood friends and then turn into adults who hang out with their families far more than their friends. Some think that it's problematic for homeschoolers to rely on their siblings, cousins, or even close friends of the family for socialization. Of course, children need to mingle with people outside of their inner circle and create connections there, but those other relationships should not be undervalued. Oftentimes, those are the friendships that last a lifetime.

FOUR:

REVAMP CHILDHOOD

Reclaiming What Belongs to Them

A child's job is to be a child, yet they are often pushed to step into unnecessary roles that defy what mother nature intended. Strict schedules, constant planned activities, and rigorous academics have gotten in the way of the season of childhood. Aside from those factors, the influence of technology and constant safety concerns from parents have hindered it as well. By using homeschooling as a way to reclaim the fundamental aspects of childhood, we can give our children an invaluable gift.

Technology Causes Kids To Grow Up Too Fast

From the lack of old-fashioned play to the simplicity of enjoying a day in the backyard, in many instances, kids today are missing out on just being a kid. Screens have taken over in almost every area of their lives, which have slowly but surely left children with little interest in the normal things that life has to offer. Calling a friend to chit-chat has been replaced with reading each other's status on social media. Using their imagination to create things has been replaced with viewing what other kids are doing on video sites. Meeting up at the park has been replaced with meeting up on a gaming platform.

Aside from the social and play aspects, kids are also attempting to look and act more grown up than they really are, speeding up the clock on childhood. Let's face it, reality TV stars, models in magazines, and celebrities have influenced preteens and teenagers for a decent amount of years. The difference now, though, is the number of influencers that exist and the constant access our kids have to them, including younger children.

Parents now have to face the challenge of guiding their children through this complex web of influences. Encouraging open dialogues about self-image and media literacy becomes crucial. By fostering an environment where kids feel comfortable discussing their online experiences, along with limiting their screen time, families can help them develop a healthy balance between their digital and real-world lives. Homeschooling can have a dramatic impact on the technology struggle. It's a little easier to set limits that differ from the rest of the crowd when that crowd is not hundreds of students. Of course, not all homeschool parents limit screen time, and I mean no judgment towards them. The point, though, is that homeschool parents can more easily live a lifestyle with their children that differs from the norm, which in this case, I'm talking about technology.

Nurturing Their Love for Nature

As a young child, many summer afternoons were spent making mud pies around a tall oak tree in my backyard. It was encased by an unkempt octagon-shaped flower bed. Sometimes, the neighborhood kids would come to play as well. I have no idea what was so exciting about that, but at the time, I think it was the ability to explore, create, and imagine anything I wanted in the natural world. Being in nature, even in my own backyard, was magical.

During my years of homeschooling, my children had much more time to enjoy the simplicity of the outdoors.

Eventhough the act of children playing outside has drastically declined over the last twenty years or so, I have found like-minded parents who are down to meet up at the park, go on mini hikes through the woods, collect rocks at the beach, et cetera. From homeschool nature clubs to the rise of forest schools, there seems to be more opportunities to throw home educated children into nature amongst other children.

In the past, children would be released from school to go home, just to run out the door again to see neighborhood friends until it was time to eat dinner, all without the effort from their parents. Today, parents now have to make it happen by offering encouragement, providing opportunities in the outside world, and modeling what we want to see by actively going out there with them sometimes.

Old-Fashioned Play

Along with the great outdoors, unstructured regular play time is dissapearing as well. It sounds unbelievable when talking about children, because playing is supposed to be what they do. For the same reasons that kids do not go outside as much, they also aren't playing as much...unless you count scrolling through social media, watching other kids play on YouTube, or switching from app to app as playing.

In order to restore old-fashioned play, parents must do some old-fashioned thinking. By "old-fashioned," you don't have to think too far back in time. Get the old board games out of the attic or set up a craft night. Incorporate some simple toys that have been loved through the generations. Promote imaginative play with items such as puppets, pretend food, or building bricks. Just because play is disappearing, you don't have to let it be that way.

Busy is Not Better

Overscheduled lifestyles lead to children who have fully packed days, leaving them with less time to just play or discover what it is they like to do on their own.

Extracurriculars are awesome to an extent, but be careful not to make the mistake of signing your children up for too much. This could mean only committing to one or two activities at a time, or even not scheduling certain activities for an entire season. Of course, as parents, we want to enrich our children's lives, but there is no need to stress them out.

As adults, we usually have to work. If we had activities constantly scheduled after work, we'd probably lose our minds. After all, everyone just wants to relax and do what we want to do. For children, their education is their "work." Let them have lots of time to unwind, be in their own company, and explore their interests that may not involve structured activities.

Sometimes, free time is the root cause of discovering a passion that one didn't know they had or never had the time to pursue before. My son has coded computer games, figured out how to rewire electronics, and built some interesting models out of random objects. My daughter has taught herself various art and craft-related skills, which led to illustration gigs and selling art in local shops and cafes.

The freedom of homeschooling gives parents an opportunity to revamp their child's life. From non-traditional school schedules to more time outside and with friends, these kids can have the ultimate school/life balance, leaving them with a fulfilled childhood.

WHAT IF INSTEAD OF DROPPING OFF OUR KIDS AT SCHOOL, WE MET UP WITH OTHER PARENTS, THE KIDS PLAYED AND EXPLORED, THEN WE WENT HOME TO EAT LUNCH, DID SOME LESSONS, AND READ BOOKS?

FIVE:

THE NITTY-GRITTY OF HOMESCHOOLING

Homeschooling Takes Commitment

Whether you are attempting to have a fully packed school day, want to live slowly and simply with your children, or are total unschoolers, homeschooling will take a certain level of commitment. Even if your family's schedule is very flexible or you are a stay-at-home parent with a lot of time to put into homeschooling, it's easier said than done when it's something that must be done on a regular basis. When it comes to home educating, it doesn't matter if you are not an expert at math, struggle with grammar, work a weird schedule, or if your children have special needs. All you need is the desire to homeschool and the willingness to commit.

Regulations & Reporting

Homeschool laws vary from state to state. Some are hands-off, and others want to stick their hands in your child's education more than what you may be fond of. Some also require annual testing, turning in portfolios, a homeschool evaluator that comes to your home, etc. There are certain states that may let you off the hook when it comes to reporting rules, such as using an accredited curriculum.

Other states, such as Michigan, are not involved at all thanks to the help of homeschooling advocates. The only requirement is to notify the school district that you are homeschooling. The state then trusts that you are appropriately teaching your child the basic subjects that they would be learning in the school system, but there are not any rules for how to go about it.

Before homeschooling, it is wise to research and familiarize yourself with your own state laws regarding home education. A reliable resource to find out this information is from the website of the Home School Legal Defense Association (HSLDA). This organization also offers memberships to any homeschool family across the country at a fair price, in exchange for any help you may need. Help offered includes getting your questions answered about homeschooling or regulations and reporting. Most importantly, HSLDA provides legal advice if your children were to ever experience discrimination, unfair treatment, or are told they cannot do something because they are/were homeschooled. They have been known to reach out to organizations or companies to make them aware that their unfair treatment or ignorance is illegal. The HSLDA has even gone as far as going to court with families. It's a handy membership to have that gives families a support system. Please note that they do not help in any way with family court situations, such as when one parent wants to homeschool but the other doesn't. Visit www.hslda.org to find your state and the home education requirements.

When Parents Don't Agree on Homeschooling

Not everyone is keen on the idea of homeschooling, which some parents might find out when they present the idea to their partner or co-parent. When that occurs, it can be devastating to realize you cannot homeschool because the other parent refuses to give their blessing. If homeschooling is that important to you, my advice is to ask them why they are against it and tell them you want specific reasons. After doing so, research topics related to their reasons and find out how homeschoolers navigate those specific challenges. For example, if the other parent is worried that their child can't participate in sports someday, find out if your district allows homeschoolers to do so. If they do not allow it, then find alternatives in the community that are not associated with the school system, such as local little league, basketball camp, or sports held by the YMCA. Once you have done your research, inform the other parent. They might budge on changing their mind or they still might not, but it's worth a try.

Another way to come to an agreement is to meet in the middle. Some schools have a "school-at-home" program. Usually, these are virtual programs done online, but the child is still allowed to attend school events and receive support from teachers. The diploma would still be issued by the school, so keep in mind that their rules and standards would have to be followed.

The Cost of Homeschooling

There seems to be a common misconception that homeschooling is only for privileged people who can afford to do so. What if I told you that homeschooling can be as expensive or as frugal as you'd like it to be? From curriculum that costs over one thousand dollars for a single child to an almost completely free approach, homeschooling is what you choose to make it. There was a time in my life when I was young and did not have the financial freedom I would have liked to have. I had to put my own curriculum together. That involved downloading free printables, checking out books from the library, looking for supplies around the house for science experiments, using online resources that were readily available, and so on.

If you're looking for a solid curriculum where everything is provided, plan on spending between one hundred to three hundred dollars per child, depending on their age. High school curriculum is usually on the more expensive end. One option is to invest more money into certain subjects and make do with cheaper or free materials for others.

Methods

Various homeschooling methods have formed over the last century. You may choose your curriculum based on the method you most wish to use, or mistakenly fall into a method because of the curriculum chosen. Many parents don't stick to a single method at all and may provide a mix of them. This method is called "eclectic," which means taking styles from many different sources and providing an array of teaching techniques.

No one method is more highly sought after than another. It all depends on the style you and your children like the most. When I was new to homeschooling, the only method I knew of was the traditional method. I thought it was necessary to create a school-at-home type of environment, from morning calendar time to memorizing facts just so they would test well. This method is what I was familiar with, after all, so I thought it was the norm. Once I read books on homeschooling and learned about other methods that existed, that's when new doors were opened up for us. I realized I had more freedom in their education.

- **Traditional Homeschooling:** this approach takes the same methods that are used in a typical classroom and then uses curriculum to closely mimic them. Many online or accredited programs use this method.
- **Classical:** this approach is similar to traditional homeschooling because it is very structured, but it differs greatly when it comes to what is taught. Classical is based on ancient educational philosophies and methods, particularly from Greece and Rome. It focuses on a challenging curriculum that emphasizes language, history, literature, and logic, with the goal of providing students with strong foundational skills and enhancing their critical thinking abilities.
- **Charlotte Mason:** a female teacher from the 1800's, Charlotte Mason is known for her soft, but thorough approach. Using literature, nature, art, music, as the forefront of a child's education, this method is meant to create great writers and thinkers, form good habits, and make them lovers of the natural world.

- **Montessori:** created by Marie Montessori, this approach emphasizes child-centered, hands-on learning, where students explore materials and engage in activities that foster their natural curiosity.
- **Waldorf:** this approach is based on the principles of Rudolf Steiner and emphasizes the importance of observing children's developmental stages and guiding learning accordingly.
- **Unschooling:** this style rejects traditional curricula and structured learning, instead allowing children to learn through their own interests and passions. Followers of this method believe that children will learn what they need to learn on their own.
- **Unit Study:** an interdisciplinary approach that involves taking a single theme or topic and integrating it into all or most school subjects. This allows the ability to dive deeper into a topic of the parent's choosing, increasing the child's understanding. Unit studies often incorporate hands-on activities such as projects or experiments.

- **Eclectic:** a flexible approach that allows parents to mix and match different homeschooling styles, methods, and resources to create a personalized education plan for their children. It's not about adhering to one specific method, but rather selecting the best elements from various approaches to cater to individual learning.

IMAGINE YOU ARE SIX YEARS OLD AND YOU MAKE BREAKFAST WITH YOUR MOM OR DAD. YOU COMPLETE YOUR LESSONS TOGETHER, ATTEND STORYTIME AT THE LIBRARY, THEN SPEND THE AFTERNOON PLAYING IN THE SUN. THIS IS HOMESCHOOLING.

SIX:

PRESCHOOL-SECOND GRADE ACADEMICS

The Curriculum is a Menu, Not a Checklist

When working through a curriculum, it's easy to get caught up in the overwhelming feeling of having to finish every last bit of it. What parents might realize, though, is that completing the entire curriculum is not needed for success. In fact, it's usually perfectly doable to omit certain assignments that you may find unnecessary, redundant, or simply do not match your child's learning style.

As I was just preparing for my son's first year of high school, I skimmed over the curriculum I bought. His language arts materials were beautifully created by the homeschool company I chose to go with. However, the literature recommended was, in my opinion, terrible. It's like the most boring books that one could possibly think of were chosen. My son already dislikes reading, so why make it seem even less fun? After receiving the language arts program, I noticed pretty quickly that it would be manageable to take out the required literature and add in my own books. Don't be afraid to make the changes that you think would work better for your child.

A Forcast of the Years Ahead

When first starting to homeschool, it's helpful to look ahead to see what the learning outcomes are for each grade level so you can see the bigger picture and how your child's education will come together in the end. However, it's important to note that not every curriculum or program will teach topics in the exact same order. Language arts and math goals are usually fairly similar, but not always. Science and history could vary greatly depending on the homeschooling method or curriculum chosen. For example, the classical method uses something called a spiral curriculum for history. Instead of moving through history in chronological order from each grade level to the next, multiple periods in history are visited in a single school year. Each year, more information is covered on the different time periods. This prevents becoming bored easily and also prevents forgetting a specific time in history because it's been so long since they last learned anything about it. Some find that this method jumps all over the place and do not like it. There's no right or wrong way; only your preferences matter.

What to Expect for Preschool

We all want the best for our kids, so preparing them as much as possible by giving them a thorough head start when they reach preschool is the greatest thing you can do, right? Wrong! Parents are so eager to jump into homeschooling and teach their children that they lose sight of what they really need...a simple foundation that includes connections with their caregiver, lots of play, time outside, and a little bit of letter and number practice.

Sing the ABCs, practice saying the sound of each letter, read books to them, and count objects. You'll also want to include a lot of sensory play that gets their hands working to improve their fine motor skills. Things like play-doh, craft making, coloring, picking up objects with tongs, or playing with sand tables can achieve this. If you do decide to give them a pencil, don't put pressure on them to write yet, as their hands are not fully developed for that.

Besides academic skills, take them to playgroups and story times to expose them to other children and adults with you safely by their side. Most of all, have fun with them.

What to Expect for Kindergarten

Kindergarten is a time when learning the sounds of each letter, number work, and handwriting gets a little more serious. They should learn the difference between upper and lower case letters, master the sound of each consonant and short vowel, memorize age-appropriate sight words, begin counting syllables in short words, and recognize their own name. Teach them that letters make words and how to sound out CVC words, such as cat and hat. Read storybooks to your kindergartner and have a conversation about it. Ask them questions about what happened to practice reading comprehension skills. Discuss what happened first, in the middle, and last in the story to practice sequencing. Then, give them a set of three steps or a simple story to put in order themselves. Work on writing each upper and lower case letter and copying simple words as well.

For mathematics, kindergarteners learn how to identify patterns and classify objects, ordinal positions such as first, second, third, and they are taught to name what comes before or after a number. Teach them the meaning of one-half by cutting sandwiches or other food items. Make up easy story problems and find the answer together. Read simple picture graphs and learn how to make one. Work on identifying coins, use a ruler to measure objects, weigh items, and talk about the volume of liquids by using measuring cups or containers. Use a thermometer to keep track of the weather and go outside to see what that specific temperature feels like. Memorize the days of the week, learn how to recognize the months of the year, and what holidays or seasons correspond. Learn the difference between right and left and also practice prepositions, such as under, over, closed, and open. Practice naming basic shapes and tracing or drawing them.

Social studies for this grade involves learning about the world around them. Talk about where they live, such as the street they live on, what's in their neighborhood, the name of their town, state, and country. Introduce them to early American history, such as Native Americans and early exploration, national symbols and monuments, and who the president is and his job. Show your child a globe and very simple maps. Learn the basic directions on a compass rose and how to use a map key.

The subject of science in kindergarten focuses on investigation skills and exploration. Teach them how to ask and answer questions on various topics. Observe the world around them, including nature or how things work. Look at science encyclopedias or books about various science topics that show good illustrations. Have fun with magnets, shadows, and gravity. Classify living and non-living things. Study plants and flowers, including how to grow something from a seed. Learn about different animals and insects and their basic features. Learn about the five senses and body parts. Talk about the Earth and its basic characteristics. Identify water, land, and the sky.

Whatever happens, don't fall into the trap of believing your child is behind if they do not catch onto every concept quickly, especially when it comes to reading. The most important thing you can do is to meet them where they are.

What to Expect for First Grade

First grade is my favorite to teach. I think it's the deeper dive into topics mixed with young curious minds that makes me excited to homeschool at this stage. They are maturing and ready for more knowledge. Language arts and math are the most important in first grade, but there's a lot of fun to be had when it comes to introducing science and social studies lessons.

First graders are usually ready to learn and recognize word patterns, word families, and root words. This helps them to decode words while reading and to be able to spell words more easily. Reading simple books with their weekly spelling words kills two birds with one stone. Aside from that, they should continue to memorize more sight words alongside normal spelling words. I like to add one or two per week to the spelling list.

For handwriting, children can practice copying age-appropriate sentences. Feel free to add spelling words to these sentences as well. Children should also be given a journal where they can practice writing their own sentences.

After giving a writing prompt, prompts can include things like: What is your favorite hobby? Who is your best friend? What did you do over the weekend? Teach your child to write a complete sentence to answer the question. You can also write a few words in a word box that they can choose from that you know would be too hard for them to spell on their own, or just to give them ideas.

Read longer books to your child and then have them answer reading comprehension questions afterward. Also, provide simple paragraphs to read together and then answer questions about the text as well. Questions should be multiple choice to start, then when they become more skilled, have them write an answer.

Basic grammar concepts can be gently introduced. Practice identifying nouns, verbs, adjectives, and proper nouns. Learn about adding "ed" or "ing" to the end of a word. Put simple words into alphabetical order. Teach the meaning of plural words and when to add "s" or "es" to make a word plural. Practice capitalization at the beginning of a sentence and ending punctuation.

Math skills build on what was previously learned in kindergarten but advance to a higher level. Counting higher, addition, and subtraction problems are the basics. By the end of the school year, they are usually learning how to add double digits without carrying over. Identifying coins now turns into memorizing their value, and then they will learn how to count and add them together. Graphs move from simple pictures to bar graphs. They will track data and record it onto a graph, along with answering questions about pre-made graphs. Teach your child how to spell numbers one through ten and how to abbreviate ordinal numbers, such as first being written as 1st. Include plenty of story problems and connect math with real life. Advance their time-telling skills by teaching the minutes on a clock and what a half an hour means. Study more types of fractions, such as one-fourth and one-third.

Social studies during this grade may include comparing the past and present, such as within the life of families.

Your child could make a family tree, look at old pictures within their own family, or listen to stories from their elders. Discuss the change in activities, clothing, or music that was once popular compared to today. Teach your child about famous people from long ago and their stories. Abraham Lincoln, Amelia Earhart, or Johnny Appleseed, for instance, are well-known American figures. Fun crafts and picture books could go well with these lessons.

Learn about holidays and the people or events associated with them, such as Martin Luther King Day and Columbus Day. Research how families around the world celebrate certain holidays differently.

Discuss Native Americans and their way of life before the U.S. became a country. Learn about tribes, their homes, and what they hunted and grew. The "new world" can also be studied. The colonial times can cover how people lived as early settlements were established. Cook old-fashioned recipes, craft toys that colonial children had, or read stories about colonial children and the family dynamics that occurred, such as how boys helped their fathers hunt and the girls helped their mothers around the house with chores.

When teaching world history, first graders usually learn about ancient civilizations, such as the Stone Age, Aztecs, and Egyptians. They study pyramids, mummies, cave paintings, nomads, now extinct mammoths, and ancient farming techniques. Geography advances from the child knowing their address and city to learning more about their state and country. The state that your child lives in can be studied by learning about the state's symbols, such as their animal, flower, and so on. Point to the state's capital city on a map and learn a little about what the governor does. It's also fun to learn about the things and people your state is famous for, the food that is made there, and any other interesting facts.

Science dives deeper into how the world works in first grade. They'll study the three states of matter and how they can change form. Outer space, including naming the planets and learning about their characteristics, is commonly explored at this time. Basic knowledge of how the Earth is rotating and its effects on the changing of the seasons and daylight is taught, along with the phases of the moon. Magnetism and electricity can be taught by playing with magnets and learning about the invention of the lightbulb. Teach about animals and their habitats, the butterfly life cycle, and the food chain of living things. Study plant life and how they need soil, sunlight, air, and water to grow and survive. This is also a good time to bring up how trees give humans oxygen, followed by environmental issues such as deforestation and pollution of the air and even the water. Children can learn about where our garbage goes and the importance of recycling. Lastly, teach your child about Earth's basic structure and landforms.

What to Expect for Second Grade

Education becomes a little more complex in second grade, moving from the basics to more advanced problem-solving, reading, and writing skills. This is also the time when independent learning is practiced. Although homeschool parents are more able to give their undivided attention to their children while they are working, it's healthy to step away during certain assignments. This allows them to mature and sets them up to succeed in their studies as they grow older.

Language arts in second grade gets into advanced decoding skills. They'll learn about syllables, word patterns, and how to properly split words up to make them easier to read. Children at this age will also naturally become better at reading aloud while correctly pausing at commas and periods, or asking questions when there is a question mark. Practicing the meaning of simple abbreviations, such as Mr. and Mrs., is also expected around this time. When it comes to reading comprehension, second graders should learn how to read a small length of text and answer questions about it or be able to find important information within it. When given fictional stories, they'll practice relaying back information about the plot, setting, and characters.

Introduce your children to a wide variety of literature: poetry, folktales, biographies, and other nonfiction or fictional stories. Make it a regular outing to visit the library or bookstore and let your children explore what interests them. You can also suggest a type of book for them to choose, but let them pick the specific one they like.

First grade is the time to learn serious handwriting skills, but second grade is the time to improve them. Provide copywork as a way to practice letters, words, and writing legible sentences. You can use handwriting-specific workbooks or let them copy from a real book.

This is a fun time to assign various types of writing projects. Together, write creative stories, reports about real things, people, or events. Throw in some simple poetry and regular journal entries. Show your children how to write a basic letter to different types of people. After practicing alongside them, ease them into independence by letting them put their ideas onto paper themselves and then helping them to edit it afterward. This way, they'll experience how to write a rough draft and polish the final copy.

For grammar skills, second graders are ready to learn more about the parts of speech, such as naming nouns, verbs, and adjectives. They'll also learn the meaning of homophones, synonyms, and antonyms. Important spelling rules that change the tense of a word are also taught during this time. For example, they'll experiment with adding "ed" or "ing" at the end of words. Show them how to make a word plural and when to add "s" or "es." Introduce the tricky words that change completely when changed from singular to plural, such as the words "man" and "men." Furthermore, teach words that stay exactly the same, such as the word "fish." Children should be getting more used to capitalizing words correctly in sentences too, such as at the beginning, proper nouns, and so on.

Regular spelling practice should continue with age-appropriate spelling lists. Practice words all week long using different methods and encourage them to master them to the best of their ability.

A big milestone for second graders is going from only addition and subtraction problems to learning the concept of multiplication. Learning the multiplication facts is crucial for the future of skills in math, but some children may struggle more than others when it comes to memorizing math facts. If this is the case with your child, you should neither keep drilling them before moving on nor should you pause where you are until they memorize them all. I have found that the best thing to do when kids are taking too long to memorize multiplication facts is to give them a cheat sheet and let them refer to it as they continue with their lessons. Guess what happens in this situation? Children will eventually memorize them on their own by looking up the answers often.

Aside from multiplication skills, second graders begin to recognize numbers up to 1000. They practice writing them in number form but may write the number words for values under 100. You'll teach them more about place values, greater and lesser than, rounding, and counting with tallies.

They'll continue to work with fractions and learn how to both recognize and write them to match up with pictures. Instead of just answering questions about bar graphs or filling them in, they'll create some by themselves with given information or by researching to collect data. Adding and subtraction will now involve carrying over and borrowing, along with working on two- and three-digit numbers. Children will also use this knowledge to add and subtract money using decimals. Tools such as balancing pans, thermometers, measuring tapes, and beakers will help your child learn how to measure and compare different types of objects by their volume, length, or weight. They'll also be introduced to various vocabulary and what kind of measurement it corresponds with, such as pounds having to do with weight and gallons measuring volume. Learning about different types of lines, such as horizontal and vertical lines, occurs during this time, along with knowing the difference between symmetrical and asymmetrical designs. They'll discover perimeter and area and how to figure out those kinds of measurements themselves. Lastly, second graders go from knowing the basic concept of the calendar to memorizing the months of the year and being able to find and locate any date on a calendar.

When it comes to history during second grade, it is the time to launch children into the making of America. They'll learn the basics of the Constitution, the Bill of Rights, and the founding fathers. They'll continue to see how the United States grew by learning about the Westward Expansion, including the pioneers who built communities, the Pony Express, the Oregon Trail, and the negative impact on the Native American tribes who were already residing on the land.

The Civil War is explored by discussing Abraham Lincoln, slavery, the Underground Railroad, and what it was like for children who were slaves, or the offspring of their parents living in slavery. They'll learn about the Yankees and the Rebels, and why they both had strong beliefs on each side of the argument.

The topic of immigration discussions in America is the "melting pot." Children get to hear about Ellis Island, the Statue of Liberty, the people who came from other countries, and what those individuals were seeking by coming to America.

World history could include places such as China or Germany. Children can learn basic knowledge about the early history of such countries, the people who live there, the cultures, and famous landmarks and symbols. Have fun exploring other countries by making crafts, cooking and trying their dishes, and reading stories based on characters who reside there.

Geography in this grade teaches children about the seven continents and the oceans. They'll learn to identify and memorize them. Additionally, they'll be able to locate the North and South Poles, the equator, and come to know the concept of longitude and latitude. Do projects such as making papier-mâché globes using a balloon, paste, newspaper, paint, and cutouts of each continent.

SEVEN:

THIRD-FIFTH GRADE ACADEMICS

What to Expect for Third Grade

By the time a child reaches third grade, they are usually reading more fluently. If for some reason they are not, evaluate the situation. Is the child just learning at their own pace? Is the child seriously struggling? Is the child showing signs of dyslexia? If you think a learning disability such as dyslexia could be present, it's important to have your child evaluated as soon as possible. If your child just seems to be struggling or is slowly moving along, he or she can still benefit from the same types of reading interventions that a child with dyslexia can. Reading curricula such as these focus on phonics and memorizing spelling rules and patterns, as opposed to just simply memorizing words as a whole. Programs such as Explode the Code or All About Reading are a couple of examples. It can be worrisome when a child is not reading as expected, but don't let yourself get caught up in the comparison game. Do what you can with the time you have when it comes to teaching your child how to read. Don't be afraid to get outside help if needed, and keep enjoying homeschooling in the process.

Third grade is a time when children can really start to enjoy the books that they are reading because they can focus more on the content rather than the process of learning to read. If your child is still struggling to read, as mentioned earlier, it might be a good idea to add in audiobooks of their choosing so that they are able to enjoy the contents of a book too. Since a child's vocabulary advances as a result of being able to read various books, that is another reason for struggling readers to listen to audiobooks. Third graders begin to answer more complex questions and summarize various kinds of text. Along with this comes the ability to advance writing skills. Children have the opportunity to take sentences and turn them into paragraphs while learning to write different kinds of pieces from persuasive to narrative paragraphs. It is also the time to crack down on punctuation, capitalization, and letter formation.

Cursive writing is a controversial topic. Some say, "Why waste time doing it?" while others cringe at the fact that many schools do not teach it anymore. Unless required by the education department where you reside, it is the homeschool parent's choice to teach cursive or not. It is most commonly taught in third grade. One benefit of teaching cursive is that it can improve handwriting skills for children who do not have very nice print handwriting. Some can write very well in cursive even though their print is not great. Maybe you'd like your children to write in cursive because you think it's an important skill or because you want their education to be well-rounded. There are no rights or wrongs; it is just a matter of preference.

Grammar skills take the same concepts as previous grades, but while taking them to the next level. As opposed to the basic parts of speech, they may learn more about things like articles and predicates. Simple sentence diagramming may be introduced as well. Children get to learn how to properly use apostrophes, such as in contractions or possessive nouns. They'll practice changing words to their past, present, or future tenses as well as identifying prefixes and suffixes of words. They'll learn the difference between complete and incomplete sentences. Lastly, spelling in third grade focuses on memorizing more sight words and spelling multisyllable words while also learning how to decode them.

Now that the foundation in mathematics has been laid, advanced multiplication problems can be taught along with the concept of division. They'll expand their knowledge of larger numbers by identifying their place value, writing in expanded and written form, comparing greater and lesser than signs, and counting high including by skip counting. They'll move on from rounding numbers to the nearest ten to rounding to the nearest hundred. Children will play around with fractions by knowing when to write them as mixed numbers. They'll compare fractions to decimals and be able to convert simple ones. It is a good idea to memorize some basic fractions and decimals such as .25 being the equivalent of 1/4. Completing larger problems related to money using decimals is also presented in multiplication, addition, and subtraction problems. Aside from bar graphs and pictographs, third graders learn how to read and create coordinate grids. They'll tell time to the nearest minute and know how to choose the correct measuring tools for various objects. Lines and angles are compared and explored. Children also learn how to calculate the circumference and diameter of a circle.

American history in third grade goes from the simple "who" and "what" questions to the "whys." Why did the American Revolution, Civil War, and Civil Rights Movement happen? Consequences of these major events may also be explored. What was it like for the people who lived through those years? For example, how did the settlers feel about the strict tax regulations required by the King of Britain? What was life like for Native Americans who had their land taken over? Why was Martin Luther King so important and what made him a great speaker?

World history puts an emphasis on exploration, including the Vikings and European explorers, and conflicts of these people showing up and taking over the land. Artists and writers from around the globe are talked about through people like Shakespeare, Leonardo da Vinci, and Beatrix Potter. Children will view samples of their work, study them, and try to replicate their styles through writing and drawing.

Geography focuses on the areas being studied during history lessons, such as routes that explorers took through the oceans of the Americas, and different parts of Europe including Spain, France, and England.

Third graders learn about a wide range of science topics including animals, plants, and ecosystems. They'll classify animals and their kingdoms, learn about photosynthesis, food chains, and the relationship between predators and prey and how they are important. Earth science covers the layers of the Earth and weather patterns. Forces and motion are studied, along with scientific laws such as Newton's law of gravitational pull. Electricity, magnetism, and properties of matter are continued topics. Forms of energy are also studied, such as thermal energy. Children use research methods, data collection, observation, experiments, and videos to learn about these science topics.

What to Expect in Fourth Grade

When children reach fourth grade, they get to use their reading skills to discover new information. Beginning research skills emerge, which allow them to look up facts for assignments, such as reports. They'll be able to locate the glossary in a book or find a specific tab on a webpage menu. The constant exposure to new vocabulary will make children better writers.

Writing lessons move beyond simple paragraphs to the five-paragraph essay. They'll learn how to brainstorm, write a topic sentence, the body, and the conclusion paragraph of different kinds of essays. Essay writing will cover opinion, informative, persuasive, and creative pieces.

Grammar studies continue to teach the parts of speech, punctuation, synonyms, antonyms, and homophones. They begin using figurative speech within their writing, including metaphors and similes.

Mathematics continues to enhance fourth graders' understanding of larger numbers, particularly in relation to place value. They also go from completing simple division problems to mastering the skill of long division. Working with fractions and decimals involves performing multiplication, division, subtraction, and addition problems. They'll explore two-dimensional shapes, symmetry, and also figure out how to determine the area and perimeter of more complex shapes. Data analysis will involve using the mean, median, and mode to measure sets of data. Measurement will focus on converting units within the metric system, understanding the concept of ratios, estimation, and probability.

Science takes fourth graders into the life of living things by exploring how they function. The human body, plants, and animals are explored. The study of outer space delves into the Moon phases, constellations, and galaxies, introducing ours as the Milky Way. Scientific investigations are conducted while children record their hypotheses, observations, and findings in a science journal. The Earth's structure is explored more closely by studying the effects of weathering and erosion, while also getting into the topic of rocks and minerals. Magnetism, electricity, matter, and forces of energy are also continued to be discussed in a more complex way.

History may start out with learning about the child's home state by studying its geographical features and its renewable and nonrenewable resources. Discussions may also cover facts about the state such as famous people, events, or what the state is known for. The history of the state can be studied by talking about the Native American tribes that first resided there and how the European settlers came about, along with the American Revolution and how it affected the early colonial life of that area. Social study topics can range from the Bill of Rights, the Constitution, the National Conventions, the United State's flag, famous songs and poems, and the important people who helped set the stage for America to become its own free country.

What to Expect in Fifth Grade

The last year before middle school is an exciting time. Increasing independence is one of the focuses of fifth grade, which can include taking more responsibility for their education. Writing notes during lessons, knowing their schedule of activities and courses, and studying on their own is common during this grade.

For reading, children tackle longer and more challenging texts, requiring them to make inferences, identify main ideas, and understand the author's purpose. They learn to analyze literary elements as well as identify and interpret figurative language that is more difficult to understand. Their knowledge of vocabulary will expand by using various methods such as dictionaries, context clues, and vocabulary study guides.

Writing advances by learning how to put together outlines, followed by creating a rough draft, editing, and completing a final draft. They'll learn how to write an interesting hook in their introductory paragraphs and also how to end the conclusion more sophisticatedly.

The topic of grammar evolves with an emphasis on the use of punctuation, particularly the appropriate application of quotation marks. Students will also learn to write from various perspectives, including first, second, and third person points of view, along with the specific grammatical rules that accompany each. A valuable teaching strategy is to provide fifth graders with paragraphs containing grammatical errors for them to correct, allowing them to apply their skills effectively.

Fifth-grade mathematics emphasizes building a solid foundation in number sense and operations, focusing on whole numbers, fractions, percentages, and decimals. Children enhance their fluency in addition, subtraction, multiplication, and division while applying these skills to solve real-world problems. Additionally, they begin to dive into more advanced concepts such as calculating the volume of geometrical shapes and also graphing and plotting with the use of coordinate planes.

Science studies focus again on physical, life, and Earth

sciences again, but while covering new topics. For example, Earth science may discuss the different levels of the sky including the atmosphere, hydrosphere, and lithosphere. The study of clouds and what they mean is also discussed more in-depth. Weather patterns, natural disasters, and climate teach children how these things are affected by Earth's systems, such as the gravitational pull of the Moon and how it causes hurricanes. Physical science presents the topic of light, sound, and heat and teaches how these kinds of energy are transferred. They'll learn about the rainbow and finally answer the question, "Why is the sky blue?" Forces and motion are discussed by teaching children about simple machines and experimenting with them by doing hands-on activities. Lastly, life science goes from learning about organisms to now observing how they interact with their environments. They'll study inherited traits, natural selection, adaptations, and learned behaviors. Fifth graders are able to see why and how living things have managed to survive.

The subject of history challenges fifth graders to research, analyze, and think for themselves when it comes to historical events. They'll use technology and books to research topics, look at geography and how it affected key events, read from primary sources, and write reports or answer essay questions. This is a good time to have discussions and debates, as well as to work on presentations independently that they'll present to you when completed. Encourage children to use various types of resources to gather information, such as watching documentaries, reading articles by historians, and looking at copies of real documents such as the Constitution. Time periods studied during this grade usually focus on the early colonization of the United States up to more modern times.

EIGHT:

MIDDLE SCHOOL ACADEMICS

Middle School No Longer Has to be Merciles

Finding classes in a hurry, remembering locker combinations, wearing the wrong clothes, or being heartlessly bullied in front of everyone no longer has to be a thing when a child is homeschooled. The anxiety that comes with middle school puts learning as a priority in the back of a lot of children's minds. It also hinders their self-esteem at a time when they could be fearlessly discovering who they are and what they are good at.

Reading

Reading skills are used to study novels that are intended for middle grades. Children should read most novels independently, but read-alouds can still be a acceptable even for older kids. My children and I had a wonderful time when I would read some books aloud. They would draw, eat their snacks, or just sit and listen intently. We could have open discussions in between, and I believe it helped them gain a love for books when they weren't always expected to do the work of reading themselves all of the time.

Although many reading lists exist for middle schoolers, I encourage parents to get creative. This is a time when children will come to the conclusion about whether or not they hate books, and it could make or break their chances of becoming a reader on their own as teens or even adults.

Also, if they are forced to read a book that they do not like, they'll be creative about how they gather the information they need to act like they have read it, either by skimming it or searching online. With that being said, parents might as well pick out novels together with their children to ensure they are interested in them. Choose a book requirement for your children, such as biographies, fantasy, or even a classic, then let them choose a specific book to read from there. Don't be afraid to let them explore non-typical genres such as graphic novels or cozy mysteries.

Literary study guides can be found online, which sometimes come in the form of actual workbooks or downloadable printables. However, many may not even exist. If you stumble upon this problem, you can either choose to make one yourself if you know the book well enough, or you can utilize other ideas. The "one-pager" is a mini report that the child makes about any book that involves writing different facts and drawing pictures to present a book on one piece of paper. Another idea is to have your child write down unfamiliar vocabulary as they read and look up their definitions after reading each chapter. Summaries can be written at the end of each chapter as well. Copywork can be assigned by picking a well-written paragraph in their book. Discuss literary elements that are used within the paragraph, such as figurative language.

Aside from reading novels, middle schoolers are expected to read informational text and pull it apart using critical thinking skills. They'll learn what it means to be biased and how to tell the difference between facts and opinions. They may also learn how to spot a credible and non-credible source when they see one. They'll be able to figure out the author's purpose and make inferences as well.

Grammar

Middle schoolers improve their grammar skills by avoiding run-on sentences and consistently using correct punctuation and sentence formation. The parts of speech are continued to be studied. They'll usually learn how to complete more complex sentence diagrams, though some homeschoolers avoid this task at a certain level because they believe it's unnecessary. Some homeschool curricula might not include too much of it when it gets to an advanced level. However, it is all a matter of the parent's preference when deciding whether to teach it or not.

Writing

The subject of writing takes middle schoolers to a new level by teaching them how to better express themselves and communicate effectively through their written work. They'll use transition techniques to make sentences and paragraphs flow better, as well as leaving out jargon in order to make a clear point and avoid meaningless words or overusage.

They'll write various kinds of essays with a clear purpose

in mind, whether they are argumentative, expository, or narrative pieces. Knowing how to tackle opposing views within their argumentative essays is also important. The study of creative writing will give them a chance to generate their own unique ideas while developing characters, settings, and plots.

Mathematics

The foundation of advanced math starts in the sixth grade. Children learn about basic algebraic expressions, ratios, rates, proportions, and how to calculate the area of different geometrical shapes. They'll work with fractions, decimals, percentages, and negative numbers. In seventh grade, children are usually ready for pre-algebra, which precedes eighth grade level algebra. This is not always the case, though, as some need more time before advancing to each level. In some cases, teens might not take pre-algebra until ninth grade, which would still technically keep them on track.

Science

Middle schoolers focus on different areas of science in each grade to better understand them. Sixth grade usually explores Earth science and astronomy. Lessons may cover the Earth's structure and plate tectonics. Space technology and exploration may be discussed, including topics related to the planet Mars. Seventh grade delves into life science. The structure of cells is explored, along with the human body systems. Animal classification and environmental topics are also learned about. Eighth grade goes over physical science, from atoms and the periodic table to the process of how chemical changes can affect matter.

Social Studies

History, civics, economics, and geography are the areas studied throughout middle school. Time periods start with ancient times such as Mesopotamia and Greece and the start of modern societies around the world. American history goes over the formation of the United States, the Declaration of Independence, the Revolutionary War, the Civil War, and reconstruction of the country. History circles back to world history when discussing the 20th century and also the United State's role in global events, such as the Cold War, the rise and fall of Adolf Hitler, and immigration in America. Geography touches base on areas discussed in regards to history. Civics teaches middle schoolers about political issues, the different parties, and current events. Economics covers the Federal Reserve, scarcity, inflation, producers and consumers, and the effect of government policies.

NINE:

ENRICHMENT STUDIES

Traditional Electives Done the Homeschool Way

When I think back to my time in elementary school, I remember having gym class twice per week and music, computer, and art class once per week. That was it. No other enrichment, no other interests being explored; we got what we got. The classes were also pretty basic, and anyone could easily tell that they lacked funding for art supplies and music lessons. With the freedom to homeschool comes the ability to transform electives into something special.

Traditional electives can be altered or added to. Technology can consist of robotics as opposed to only sitting at a computer, learning how to copy and paste. Art can be approached with more creativity or the use of other art forms such as digital drawing, photography, or pottery wheel throwing. Gym can make use of any physical activity imaginable. Life skills can take children outside of a classroom and expose them to real-life activities, such as changing a tire or planning a party. Special interests can be explored by turning them into an elective class as well, such as magnet fishing, hunting, or crocheting.

Art

For younger grades, traditional art class usually consists of premade templates being handed out to students. They closely follow the step-by-step instructions of the art teacher until there is a finished product that looks the same as everyone else's. Occasionally, they might have the opportunity to throw in creativity when painting an object they made out of clay.

In middle and high school, assignments are closely followed, but students may get to put their creativity to work a little more. When one of my children attempted to participate in elective classes at our local high school, she was unhappy with the art class. All of the students were instructed to use laptops to read art lessons and take quizzes online while the teacher sat quietly at his desk. By the end of the first week, she never even got out a pencil to draw something.

As homeschool parents, we sometimes have these intrusive thoughts about the education they might be missing out on. We worry that we might not provide one that is enriching enough, when really homeschool parents have the upper hand when it comes to this. We don't have to stick to strict assignments that are usually used to manage a full classroom. We can instead travel off the regularly taken path, creating something unique for our children.

Experimenting with different mediums and skill levels can happen from a young age. Haul the easel outside and have your child paint a still life of nature. Sign them up for a mosaic class at your local art studio. Let them participate in art contests if that interests them. Have them choose an art skill they'd like to gain and pick up the supplies to do so. There are endless options.

Music

Throughout a child's school years, it's common for them to learn about music appreciation, basic music note reading skills, the names of instruments, some classical musicians, and they may even learn how to play a simple instrument such as the recorder. I love how homeschooling can tailor music class so that it's customized for the child. From exploring music genres and artists to having a choice of what instrument the child wants to learn, they are able to gain experiences in music that are possibly far greater than what a typical education has to offer.

When it comes to teaching children how to play an instrument, of course, paying for private lessons is an option. However, with the advancement of technology, children can learn how to play many instruments at home without parents having to pay large amounts of money or having any knowledge of that instrument themselves.

DON'T STRIVE TO COPY A SYSTEM YOU CHOSE TO TAKE YOUR CHILD OUT OF.

Music appreciation is able to leave the realm of typically shared music available within schools. Classic rock, indie bands, worship music, or today's pop music can be explored, putting a unique spin on homeschooling music class.

Studying the notes played within songs, the history of certain kinds of music, or even the biographies of artists are all examples.

Physical Fitness

Physical education or "P.E." focuses mostly on physical activities that get children moving, but it can also include some book work, such as when studying nutrition. Some states require that homeschoolers log a certain number of hours completing physical tasks, so be sure to check your state's requirements before assigning a P.E. class. Physical activities for P.E. can range from structured activities, such as using a curriculum that guides children on what to do, to laid-back activities like skateboarding. Some might take advantage of organized classes, such as those offered by a yoga studio, at a co-op, or sports offered at the YMCA. Joining a community club, such as a roller derby team, is another option. Parents may also let their child choose a physical activity that they would like to practice, and even excel at, such as BMX.

Life Skills

What better place to learn life skills than a homeschool environment? Typically, areas of study include topics such as financial literacy, homemaking, auto care, or internet safety. I often hear others ask, "Why don't kids learn this or that in school?" Usually, they are talking about life-related skills like growing food, understanding taxes, or starting a lucrative business. Homeschooling allows children to go deeper into topics such as those that have a meaningful affect on their education. It also allows for more hands-on activities that bring real skills to life.

Foreign Language

Depending on the school system, foreign language is taught in different ways. Many offer classes in middle school, and most require that high schoolers earn one or two credits learning a second language as well. Some might even incorporate the teaching of a new language as young as kindergarten, such as Spanish or sign language. Even though learning a foreign language is a common part of public or private education, it usually can't be customized to fit the desires of the students, and the offerings may be limited. Homeschooling, on the other hand, offers a unique opportunity to tailor language education to the interests and needs of each child. Parents can introduce languages that align with their cultural heritage, future travel plans, or even career aspirations. This personalized approach not only makes learning more engaging but also helps children develop a deeper appreciation for different cultures and perspectives.

In a homeschool setting, language learning can be integrated into everyday activities, making it a natural and enjoyable part of life. For example, cooking a traditional dish from a country where the target language is spoken provides a hands-on learning experience that reinforces vocabulary and cultural understanding. Additionally, homeschooling allows for the use of diverse resources, such as online platforms, language exchange partnerships, and multimedia content, which can enhance the learning experience and provide exposure to native speakers.

Technology

The study of technology can be explored in various ways, from basic computer skills such as typing and software programs, to the mastery of more advanced skills like webpage design and coding. Whether a child wants to learn only the basics, or they are interested in diving deeper into the world of technology, many programs and curriculum exist to make it happen right from home.

Resources to Explore:
- Scratch
- Code Academy
- ID Tech
- Outschool
- Roblox Studio & Minecraft
- Tynker

Additional Enrichment

When homeschooling, any interests and passions can be studied, whether it is used as an elective or as extra enrichment for a child's education.

Enrichment Ideas:

- nature study
- survival skills
- blacksmithing
- fiber arts
- drama
- gardening
- bread making
- photography
- STEM
- community service projects
- book club
- wood working
- stop motion
- book binding
- cake decorating
- play writing

TEN:

HIGH SCHOOL & GRADUATION

The Future Looks Different for Everyone

When a parent tells someone that they homeschool, a common question asked is, "But you'll send them to high school, right?" Our society is very stuck on the idea that high schoolers must attend "real" school and that anything different is absurd. There are a few main reasons why these beliefs exist.

First off, the academics are obviously more difficult, making some individuals believe that parents are not capable of homeschooling at that level. That is a huge myth. With the resources that are available in today's world, children can successfully be homeschooled at any grade level. Whether parents take advantage of easy-to-use curriculum, utilize online videos, courses, or outsource certain subjects to tutors when a parent does not feel comfortable, there are plenty of options.

The typical high school experience is the other reason why many think that teens should not be homeschooled. In fact, it seems that people are actually more concerned with this matter than the academic portion. From sports and the marching band, to pep rallies, and homecoming dances—how do homeschooled teens have fulfilling lives without these things? The first step is realizing that these aspects of high school are actually a tiny portion of the four years of high school.

If you have a teen who wishes to participate in a lot of sports or any at all and there are not other sports-related teams to join, such as community recreational leagues or those organized by a private entity like homeschool co-ops, then considering sending your child to high school might be something to think about. However, many teens don't participate in sports at all or aren't that interested in them to the point where it is a top priority. If that's the case, then maybe don't let that be a factor that outweighs homeschooling.

Dances such as homecoming and prom are exciting events for teens, but are they exciting enough to forget homeschooling as a result? Keep in mind that these school events happen once or twice per year, depending on the grade the teen is in. Additionally, with the rise of homeschooling, it may be possible to find a formal dance event in your area that is exclusively for homeschoolers. Usually, events like these are put on by homeschool co-ops, a group of homeschool parents, or possibly even a church.

The high school experience we all think of in our heads does not have to look the same for everyone. It can be just as wonderful, or possibly even better depending on the person's perspective. The question is, what kind of life does your homeschooled teen want to have? We'll explore in detail how to homeschool at this level, and how to make it amazing.

Requirements for Graduation

In order for a homeschooler to graduate high school, parents must first know what the guidelines are in their residing state. Requirements for graduation vary greatly across the country, but many states do not require homeschoolers to follow the same rules that public and private schoolers do, leaving it up to the parents to determine when their teen has successfully completed high school. If this is the case, parents usually create the plan for high school, make the transcript, and even issue a diploma. Doing so would be completely legit, meaning that the student really *did* graduate and that all entities within that state must accept their diploma as a credible document, including colleges and employers. However, it is a wise idea to still mimic the general requirements as your local school district, especially if your teen plans on going to college. Doing so, though, doesn't hinder the unique spin that you can put onto their classes.

Some states have strict laws for graduation, such as turning in portfolios, or making the student take standardized tests. In a few states such as New York, even more rules must be followed.

The Transcript

High school graduation is usually determined by the number of credits given to the student. A common number of credits to achieve is 26. In many cases, one credit is awarded for each class taken throughout the school year, and half a credit is awarded for a class that lasts a shorter amount of time, such as half of a school year. The classes that high schoolers take can vary, especially for homeschoolers. Typically though, over the course of their four-year high school career, they will have completed four English classes, three to four science classes, three to four math classes, three to four history classes, and various electives. To keep track of your teen's classes, credits, and grades, you'll record them on a document called a transcript. It's like an official version of a report card. You can create this document from scratch using a software program, or you can use a transcript service that is available online. This type of service makes it easy to add in the student's information and create a seamless finished document. It can even determine the cumulative G.P.A. based on the grades that you enter. An example of a homeschool transcript is available on the next page.

HIGH SCHOOL TRANSCRIPT

(Grades 9-12)

Graduation Date: 06/01/2024

School of Record
Homeschool Name, If Applicable
Homeschool Parent's Name
Home Address
Parent's Email

Student Information
Student's Name
Gender
Date of Birth
Address
Phone
Student's Email

9th Grade 2020-2021	Grade	Credits
English 9	A-	1
Pre-Algebra	B	1
US History	A	1
Biology / Lab	B+	1
American Sign Language I	A	.5
Online Experience: Digital Art	A	1
American Sign Language II	A	.5
GPA = 3.67		6

10th Grade 2021-2022	Grade	Credits
English 10	A	1
Algebra I	B-	1
World History	A	1
Chemistry	B	1
American Sign Language III	A-	.5
Mixed Media Art	A	1
American Sign Language IV	A	.5
GPA = 3.59		6

11th Grade 2022-2023	Grade	Credits
English 11	A	1
Geometry	B	1
Civics	A-	.5
Agricultural Science	A	1
Physical Education	A	.5
Life Skills	A	1
Economics	A	.5
Health Education	A	.5
GPA = 3.81		6

12th Grade 2023-2024	Grade	Credits
English 12	A	1
Algebra II	C	1
Art History	A	1
Environmental Science	A	1
Career Exploration	A	1
Fiber Arts	A	1
GPA = 3.67		6

Summary By Grade

Grade	9th	10th	11th	12th
Cum. GPA	3.67	3.63	3.69	3.68
Credits Earned	6	6	6	6

Cumulative Summary (9th - 12th)

Total Credits	GPA Credits	GPA Points	GPA
24.00	24.00	88.40	3.68

Authorized Signature   Date: 06/01/2024

English Language Arts

Throughout high school, teens usually take a language arts class each year. These classes are most commonly called English one, two, three, and four. Each English course includes the analysis of literature. The literary elements are explored, written text is carefully examined, and students are guided on how to form well-supported arguments about it. Learning how to analyze literature broadens their understanding when they read and makes them better researchers and writers. Aside from learning about literary analysis, high schoolers should be exposed to various types of genres of novels.

Middle school laid the foundation for high school writing skills, but now students will continue to polish them. They'll write advanced essays that include backing their writing with research, citing their sources, and making well-thought-out arguments, points, or themes. They'll practice writing a promising hook that reels in the reader and also end their essay with a bang. Aside from writing a good essay, creative writing is also explored through poetry, short stories, or other forms. Students get to learn about what elements make a good story and how to utilize them within their own writing.

On top of progressing their writing skills, high schoolers have the opportunity to hone their speaking skills. Through presentations, discussions, debates, and projects, students use their voice as opposed to only their pencil. Practicing speaking skills enhances verbal communication and prepares them for different areas of their lives, such as in college, their career, involvement in community organizations, or even when speaking on personal matters.

Lastly, good grammar is still studied throughout high school using various examples and providing plenty of opportunities to practice their knowledge of correct grammar usage. High schoolers should be able to effectively use their grammar skills within writing assignments and recognize basic errors in other written texts.

When planning your teen's language arts classes, remember that it is okay to veer off the common path if it's allowed in your state to do so. For example, one year of language arts might not look like a typical English class that includes all of the topics like reading, writing, grammar, etc. One whole course could be creative writing only if that's what your teen is really interested in. Generally, homeschooling makes it possible to tweak your teen's classes in any way you like.

Mathematics

Depending on what level of math your teen is ready for will determine the type of math they take in high school. If they successfully finish pre-algebra, they would take Algebra I in ninth grade, geometry in tenth grade, algebra II in eleventh grade, and then there is usually an option to take more advanced math in twelfth grade or take an alternative class, such as personal finance. If your teen struggled in middle school and you feel that they are not ready for Algebra I, then there is some room to be able to take pre-algebra in ninth grade and algebra in tenth grade. Then they could take geometry in eleventh grade, and algebra two in twelfth grade. If going this route, the student would be considered to have completed all necessary math classes depending on the state that they reside in. If your teen is ahead in math or advances quickly through classes, that would leave more room for advanced classes such as trigonometry. If you are worried that your teen will not complete the necessary math classes by the end of twelfth grade, consider using a curriculum such as *Learn Math Fast*. It is a simplified, easy-to-use curriculum for any grade level that gets to the point quickly and can be finished in a shorter amount of time than a traditional math program.

Science

Generally, high schoolers take biology, chemistry, physics, and one other science course of their choice. This can vary depending on your state's guidelines or your student's preferences. For example, in Michigan public schools, it is required that students take biology as their first class, then they can choose to take either chemistry or physics in tenth grade. For their third year, students can choose any type of science course, such as life science, agricultural science, or astronomy. They also have the option to add another science course in twelfth grade if they choose, or if they need another credit to graduate. If a homeschooler resides in Michigan, they could choose to mimic the same layout of classes, or they could take any science classes they prefer since it is not required by their state to follow the same exact plan.

If you are a parent who is concerned about not having the correct or expensive supplies to teach high school science, just know that there are many resources available. Science lab kits that are affordable can be shipped right to your door, such as frog dissection kits. If you do not want to buy supplies for every lab, online resources are available as well that show videos of the lab being completed that your high schooler follows along with. There are also online interactive labs that can be completed digitally.

Social Studies

The most commonly taken social studies classes in high school are American history and world history along with corresponding geography. After that, civics is taken during one semester and economics taken during another semester in the same academic year. A fourth class is usually optional in twelfth grade. Sometimes, a geography class can be a standalone class as well if preferred.

History courses dive much deeper at the high school level. Historical events are closely examined, and critical thinking is encouraged. Geography allows students to gain a better understanding of the world by exploring many different regions within their own continent as well as around the globe. Civics teaches students about the government and how it is run. Economics teaches them about how the government affects the economy, both in business and the impact on the average American citizen.

Electives

In chapter nine, the choices for electives were discussed

and the same information applies to high schoolers as well. The only other aspect to think about is whether or not certain electives are required to graduate, or if you are following the same guidelines as your public school system. If choosing to follow certain guidelines, in most cases the content of each class is totally up to the parent. For example, if you want to include physical education and there are not any strict rules about what is taught within that course, then feel free to create the kind of course you want. This could look like counting karate or dance classes as a credit. It could include time spent at a local gym using a membership. If creating a whole fitness plan that includes various exercises or meeting a specific fitness goal such as a certain number of minutes per week exercising, that is an option too.

    High school is a great time to test out new interests by turning them into electives. A teen that is interested in learning how to sew or tailor clothing could practice that skill by turning it into an art-related class.

Dual Enrollment

Dual Enrollment involves a high school student being enrolled part-time in either a community college or possibly a university. A benefit of dual enrollment is working towards a college degree while also counting college classes as high school credits. The option to participate can look different depending on the state. Some allow homeschoolers to easily enroll. Others might first require the student to go through the public school system, meaning they have to enroll as a part-time student and then apply for a dual enrollment program. In some states, that might mean taking a certain number of classes, such as electives, at their local school in order to qualify. Another factor to take into consideration is the cost. Some states provide funds for homeschoolers to join in on dual enrollment, while others refuse to pay for it or might only do so if they are enrolled part-time in a public or private school.

Vocational Technical Schools

Technical schools offer high schoolers a pathway to a

career. Either by gaining skills to use for the future or by working towards an actual certification of some kind that the student will be able to jump into employment with. Many technical schools provide a tuition-free education while others do not, but in many cases still offer financial aid. Some examples of technical school programs are cosmetology, welding, or computer programming.

Apprenticeships & Job Shadowing

Homeschooling frees up time for high schoolers to be able to use their time in ways that typical students cannot. Apprenticeships at real job sites may be available to willing teens who have the time in their day to learn alongside their regular schoolwork. It could also be worth reaching out to companies or organizations that have job roles that the teen is interested in to see if they can job shadow an employee for a day or even a week. This would allow them to observe the day in the life of that kind of role, let them ask specific questions, and potentially get their foot in the door for the future.

Working While in High School

Like students enrolled in traditional schools, homeschoolers are allowed to work and earn a paycheck as long as they obtain a work permit. However, states may require that homeschoolers follow the same work laws as public or private school students. This means that working during certain hours of the day may still not be prohibited, even if homeschoolers have a more flexible schedule. Some locations could be strict about this, while others might let homeschoolers choose their school hours, meaning they could technically have school hours during the evenings so they can work during the day. It's possible, though, that the work permit states the exact times the student can and can't work, regardless of what their homeschool schedule is like.

The Diploma

As mentioned before, many states allow parents to issue a

high school diploma themselves. If they do not, that is most likely because the law is stricter and may have required the student to be enrolled in an accredited homeschool program, which would usually issue a diploma to the student instead. When parents are responsible for the diploma, one can be made by using a similar online service as when making the transcript, or one can be created using a computer program. When it comes to the time to do so, make sure to state the issuing date and two witnesses who will sign off on the diploma. These witnesses could be both parents or anyone else in addition to the main individual who homeschooled the teen, unless otherwise noted by their residing state. A sample of a homeschool diploma is below:

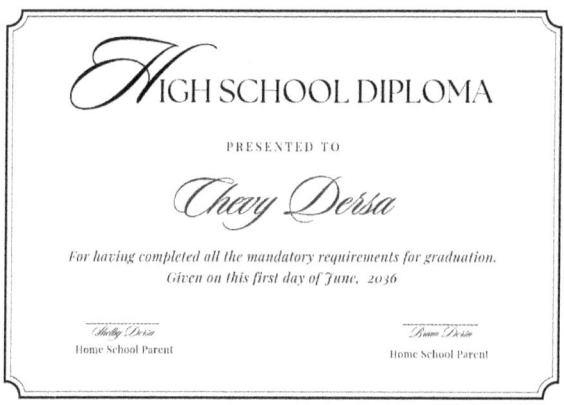

ELEVEN:

CREATE A HOMEMADE EDUCATION

Your Homeschool Mission

Everyone has a "why" when initially deciding to homeschool. What starts out as one reason, though, often turns into many after they have taken the leap. I was once a mom just looking to help my child who was struggling in school with dyslexia. I thought that I would send her back after a couple of years of specialized tutoring and working with her one-on-one. However, I soon found myself with more reasons to keep homeschooling. The goal I had in the first place turned into a homeschooling mission. Mine was no longer just about a good education; it was about a better childhood. The days of being a child are short, and homeschooling allows more time to enjoy them.

When thinking about your homeschool mission, don't be afraid to go in full force. Doubts will come from many directions, including your own inner thoughts. Keep your reasons for deciding to homeschool in mind and remember that nothing has to be proven to anyone. That will set you free and allow you to focus on your family and your homeschooling purpose.

What are Your Reasons?

- Promote positive peer interactions
- Eliminate bullying
- Enhance the quality of their education
- Slow down childhood
- Simplify childhood
- Family time
- Free time
- Flexibility
- Address learning needs
- To achieve specific goals
- To help their future as an adult or in their career

List Your Reasons:

Mission Statement Sample

Our homeschool mission is to put childhood at the center of everything we do. We will rid our lives of unnecessary tasks and replace them with meaningful ones whenever possible. We will not compare our academic education with that of others, but create one with only our needs in mind.

By fostering a nurturing and supportive environment, we aim to inspire curiosity and a lifelong love of learning. Our focus will be on developing critical thinking skills, creativity, and resilience in our children. We commit to celebrating individuality and encouraging each child to explore their unique interests and talents. Collaboration, empathy, and respect will be the cornerstones of our educational approach, as we prepare our children to contribute positively to the world around them.

Write Your Homeschool Mission Statement

What are Your Methods?

- Charlotte Mason
- Montesorri
- Traditional
- Classical
- Waldorf
- Unit Study
- Unschooling
- Eclectic
- Secular or religious-based
- Online, books only, or both

List Your Methods:

State Laws & Regulations to Remember

Curriculum to Explore & Details About Each One

- _____
  _____
  _____
- _____
  _____
  _____
- _____
  _____
  _____
- _____
  _____
  _____
- _____
  _____
  _____

Keep it Simple & Make it Magical

Children are easily amazed by the world around them. They can remind us adults how the simple things are the best things. Although it might seem nice, it's not necessary to have the top-of-the-line curriculum, a fully decorated homeschool room, or every fancy online course that is advertised. Kids are happy that they get to eat a slow breakfast with you, have you help them when they struggle, and get to learn more about things that interest them.

Whether you and your children are discovering raspberries while on a nature walk, reading a book together that you both can't wait to get back to, or working together to grasp a new math concept and it finally clicks for them, those are the things that make homeschooling magical. An education does not have to be rigorous for it to count. It just takes an invested parent, some time out of each day, and the philosophy of a homemade education.

The Philosophy of a Homemade Education

HOME IS THE MOST IMPORTANT PLACE

NEVER BE AFRAID TO REBEL AGAINST A BROKEN SYSTEM

LIBRARY CARDS ARE A USEFUL TOOL

STRIVE TO PRESERVE CHILDHOOD

CONVERSATIONS CAN SOMETIMES BE THE BEST LESSONS

THE CURRICULUM IS A MENU, NOT A CHECKLIST

SIMPLE IS MAGICAL

www.ingramcontent.com/pod-product-compliance
Lightning Source LLC
Chambersburg PA
CBHW070202100426
42743CB00013B/3012